Tasting

**For a free color catalog describing Gareth Stevens' list of high-quality books,
call 1-800-542-2595 (USA) or 1-800-461-9120 (Canada).
Gareth Stevens' Fax: (414) 225-0377.**

Library of Congress Cataloging-in-Publication Data

Pluckrose, Henry Arthur.
    Tasting/by Henry Pluckrose; photographs by Chris Fairclough.
        p. cm. -- (Exploring our senses)
    Includes bibliographical references and index.
    ISBN 0-8368-1290-5
    1. Taste--Juvenile literature. [1. Taste. 2. Food. 3. Senses
and sensation.] I. Fairclough, Chris, ill. II. Title. III. Series.
QP456.P56   1995
612.8'7--dc20   94-41622

North American edition first published in 1995 by
Gareth Stevens Publishing
1555 North RiverCenter Drive, Suite 201
Milwaukee, Wisconsin 53212, USA

Additional Photographs: Peter Millard 4, 22, 24, 28.

EXPLORING OUR SENSES

Tasting

By Henry Pluckrose
Photographs by Chris Fairclough

Gareth Stevens Publishing
MILWAUKEE

How do we taste things?

4

What things
do you like
tasting most?

5

Do you like the sharp, sour taste of grapefruit?

Or do you prefer the sweet, sticky taste of honey and jam?

**Do you like
the hard, dry taste
of crackers?**

Or do you prefer
the creamy, soft taste
of whipped cream?

Our favorite food
is the one we enjoy
tasting the most.
Is yours crusty bread . . .

or a crunchy apple?

11

Is it hard nuts . . .

or moist cake?

Do you like the crunchy taste of raw carrots?

Which vegetables
do you like best?

15

Do you like
the juicy taste
of pineapple?

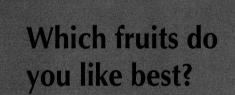

Which fruits do you like best?

17

There are some things we do not want to taste. Some medicines taste unpleasant . . .

and so does soap.

19

Some things taste unpleasant when they are raw.

They taste good
when they are
freshly baked.

Try to imagine the taste
of ice cream . . .

or eggs.

Can you describe
the taste of
bananas . . .

or candy?

Some foods taste best served hot.

Other foods taste best served cold.

Do you enjoy the taste of creamy milk?

Do you like
the coolness
of ice water?
Does water have
a taste?

Do you like the warmth of a hot drink before bedtime?

Remember —
the last taste to
enjoy each night
is the clean taste
of toothpaste!

More Books to Read

Tasting. Kathie B. Smith (Troll)
Teach Me about Tasting. Joy W. Berry (Childrens Press)
Touch, Taste, and Smell. Steve Parker (Watts)

Videotape

You and Your Sense of Smell and Taste. (Disney)

Activities for Learning and Fun

1. Tea Time You can change the taste of tea by adding small amounts of honey, sugar, lemon juice, cinnamon, or other ingredients. Mix a glass of plain instant iced tea, following the directions on the jar. Taste the tea, then add a sweetener or flavoring of your choice. How has the taste changed? Do some "market research" to find out which tea most of your friends prefer. Let them sample the plain tea first, then add one or more different sweeteners or flavors of your choice. Which is most popular?

2. Hey, Bud! The taste buds on your tongue blend flavors of foods that are salty, sour, sweet, or bitter. Try this simple experiment to learn more about your taste buds and where they are located. Dip an unsalted pretzel into some honey. Touch different parts of your tongue with the honey, from front to back and side to side. Do some areas of your tongue respond more to the sweet taste of the honey than other areas? Repeat the experiment with something salty, something sour, and something bitter.

Index